Estate Sale DIY

how to run your own estate sale instead of paying someone else to do it

Annie Smidt

In memory of Susan Smidt 1937-2019

Estate Sale DIY: how to run your own estate sale instead of paying someone else to do it
by Annie Smidt
©2020 All rights reserved

Special thanks to Ilana Schwartz.

For additional information and resources, please visit **estatesaleDIY.com**

Contents

Introduction

There are a number of reasons why you might hold an estate sale. Probably the most common reason is the eponymous one: the dissolution and dispersal of an estate after a death or legal issue. An estate sale could also be held on account of other life changes: downsizing, moving to assisted living, moving overseas, divorce, etc. The common denominator is that (pretty much) everything must go.

While estate sales are sometimes indicative of exciting times in your life — like selling most of everything in your empty nest home to downsize and move closer to family and grandchildren — commonly, they are more mandated than voluntary and come with stressful situations.

Taking on a huge task like an estate sale while caring for aging parents, dealing with their recent loss, or fighting one of the various kinds of estate-related legal battles can be overwhelming at best.

Most people, when faced with this seemingly herculean task, will immediately think to call in the experts and head to Google to find local estate sale companies. I'm not trying to dissuade you from doing this. There are lots of cases where it's the best way to go.

Reading, or even skimming this book will give you an idea of whether or not you have the bandwidth to do it yourself or if you'd rather hand it over to people who run estate sales on the regular. If you do decide to hire pros[1], I would encourage you to seek out personal recommendations as your first tactic. At the least, check out any potential estate sale companies on Yelp, other review sites, or with the Better Business Bureau. There are definitely differences in quality, style, and scrupulosity in this industry. Also, interview a few different companies for comparison. And trust your gut.

But this is not really the topic at hand. Let's talk DIY.

You might choose to run your own estate sale instead of paying someone else to do it. Possible reasons why include:

---

1 Although this book assumes a you can hold an in-person estate sale, in times of pandemic-related safety concerns, you may need to move to an online-model or get more help from a professional estate-sale company than you might normally have chosen to. For a discussion of different options you can pursue when social distancing necessary, check out the Afterword.

- You are a do-it-yourselfer and it seems the natural choice
- You want or need the money you'd save by not handing over a cut to an estate sale company (typically 35%-50% of sales plus extra fees for various services)
- You (or your relative) is actually living in the property during the time the prep for the sale would take place and you don't want the constant intrusion of strangers all over the house

I won't lie to you. Running your own estate sale is a lot of work. I honestly wouldn't undertake it unless you're feeling motivated. If the idea of being enthused about such a project sounds like nonsense to you, please just hire professionals. You'll be much happier in the end.

If, on the other hand, you think running your own estate sale sounds fun and rather satisfying and you're excited to make more money and not have to deal with an outside company, read on.

> **WHAT THIS BOOK IS NOT**
>
> This is not a book about how to form an estate sale company. It's for individuals and families who want or need to hold a one-off or occasional event.

Part one: Assessing

What do you want to get out of it?

As with any project, it's important to know your ultimate goal from the beginning. Figure out what you want to get out of this — then set your own expectations and perhaps those of a parent or other relative you're doing this for. Common goals are:

- Make the maximum profit
- Get the stuff out of your life
- Get the stuff to those who need it
- A hybrid of the above, or something else

Your goal(s) may affect the choices you make going through the process, so it's good to be clear from the outset.

Getting the stuff out of your life or getting the stuff to people in need

If profit isn't your primary goal and a liquidation of physical assets is not mandated by legalities, you might want to take an entirely different approach and do the whole process backward. In other words, you should start with the disposal and donation methods described in The Aftermath section, and then run a sale with whatever is left. With any luck, you won't even have enough left to bother with a sale, and if you do, it won't even be a full-fledged estate sale — more like a yard sale. Or, you could just get a dumpster or junk removal service to haul away everything that's left and call it a day.

What do you have?

Keepers

Literally, take a look around. Are there things that you want or need to keep? (For the sake of simplicity going forward, assume "you" means you or someone you're holding a sale for). This will be quite different if the sale is because of a death versus downsizing or other more voluntary life changes. In the former case, everything — or very close to it — will likely need to go. In the latter case, there will probably be a lot of personal items you are planning to keep.

Make a list (on paper or mentally) of what you are not selling. This can be at a fairly macro-level at this point: "Clothes in Mum's bedroom closet", "Dad's Laz-E-boy", etc.

Remember, "what you're not selling" may include the things you're keeping personally, items which family members wish to take as keepsakes of a deceased person, and borrowed items which need to be returned to their real owner (the cable company, the library, a friend, etc.).

Consider what's left to be sold. It's still enough to bother having an estate sale, right? If not, consider something more like a yard sale or getting a charity truck to come by. If you are still ready to go for an estate sale, read on.

Fair game items

Now focus on what will be in the sale. If it helps you to visualize the scope and character of what you've got, make a list at a macro level, noting anything that seems especially valuable/desirable (e.g. books in office, mom's gold jewelry, bedroom furniture, kitchen stuff, garage stuff, dad's model planes, etc.).

People will really buy that?
Don't second guess what people will and will not buy at an estate sale at this point, especially if you've never been to one yourself. You will probably be surprised. Amongst other things, the following items are potentially sellable:

- Sealed packages of health and beauty products (mouthwash, makeup, shampoo, etc.)
- Sealed or unsealed household products, even half-empty packages (cleaners, potting soil, sponges, etc.)
- Sealed or unsealed (even half-used) bottles of perfume
- Sealed non-perishable food items and liquor[2]
- Used clothes, shoes, and accessories (any size, brand, era, style)
- Used and unused office supplies

---

2 Technically, it may not be legal to sell these items without a license where you live and there may be a higher level of liability risk than with other items, so proceed with your own good. judgment

- Old gadgets and tech (even very old)
- Houseplants (mature plants sell can sell for big bucks)
- Old magazines
- Totally random junk in your basement, attic, and garage
- Somewhat broken furniture
- Costume (fake, "junk") jewelry
- Old kitchenware
- Washer, dryer, fridge[3]
- Window treatments
- Used towels and linens
- Fancy doorknobs attached to your doors, nice switchplates, cabinet hardware, etc.[4]

But probably not...

The *general* rule of thumb is don't throw things out because you think they won't sell. You can, however, feel free to dispose of items which are:

- Literally trash
- Gross (moldy, smelly, stained, bug-infested, full of mouse poop, etc.)
- Non-working and unlikely to be fixed/fixable (cheap gadgets, appliances)
- Missing significant pieces that are difficult or not worth replacing (jigsaw puzzles, appliances)

Hard-to-sell items

Just like it's a little weird what people *will* buy, the items that are hard to move can be a little counterintuitive. Here are a few categories:

- **Non-rare books and cookbooks.** Even if they're great, you'll probably only sell a small percentage of what you have.
- **Expensive furniture.** Some can move at high-end sales, but furniture is hard to resell these days and people buying for

---

3 If you're going to sell the house after the sale, check with your realtor as to whether this is a good, bad or indifferent idea in your situation.

4 This is usually only relevant for demolition sales when the property is going to be torn down.

personal tend to want good deals on functional pieces rather than fanciness.

- **Out-of-style furniture.** Sometimes bargain-hunters looking for function over form will grab this up if it's priced right, but it also may be really tough to convince anyone they need your grandma's 70s orange-vinyl-upholstered dining room set.
- **Collectibles that used to be popular.** At the moment (2020) it is hard to sell (or sell for very much) Hummels, Lladros and various other ceramic and porcelain figurines, bone china, sets of fancy dishes, sets of flatware (silver or plate), crystal and similar items that used to be sought after. Or at least decent wedding gifts. Oh, and Beanie Babies.

Strategic decisions

After this high-level assessment of what you have, your next steps will probably depend on your goals:

- If you are looking to make the maximum profit (and are not legally obligated to sell everything in a public/estate sale), you may want to read the next section about how and where to sell certain items *before* the estate sale.
- If you have to, or want to, sell everything in one big sale, skim the next section, then jump in at "Part Two: Researching prices" on page 33.
- If your priority is to get items to people who need them and sell or junk what's left, check out "Part Five: After the sale" on page 77.

Selling things everywhere *except* an estate sale

If your strategy is to sell everything for as much as possible, you may want to try to sell certain items before the sale in specific ways. (If that's unsuccessful, you can add the items back into the sale).

Estate sale shoppers are generally looking for bargains, and a good percentage of them will be looking for items they can purchase and then resell themselves and make a profit. Because of this, there are price points where you're just not going to be able to sell items at an estate sale — regardless of their fair market value or what you perceive their worth to be.

To a degree, the prices you can charge will depend on factors like the overall fanciness of the neighborhood, the upscale or downscale nature of house itself, and the quality of the goods in the sale. If the location is a ritzy area and you have a house filled with high-end and designer items, you'll be marketing the sale to buyers who are looking for that sort of thing and will have expectations of higher prices. They may be in the market for an antique silk rug, or a piece of Louis Vuitton luggage and will be happy to buy that one item at half of the retail price.

If your sale is more of a hodgepodge, or if the property and area are more middling or humble, you'll be marketing a different way and buyers will be expecting cheaper prices. This isn't necessarily a bad thing. They are likely to buy more in bulk. We'll talk more about these different kinds of sales and their ramifications later on in the book.

It's all good. You have the items you have. Let's figure out how to sell them for the most money. This can be a balancing act between profit and effort, so go through the suggestions and tackle as much as you feel up for.

You may have identified items while you were assessing which would bring in more profit if sold somewhere other than an estate sale. These are chiefly:

- Jewelry and watches
- Collectibles
- Art
- Clothing and accessories

We'll look at each one more closely.

Jewelry and watches

Real jewelry

If you have real jewelry — gold, silver, diamonds, high-quality gemstones by high-end makers (Cartier, Bvlgari, Van Cleef & Arpels, Fabergé, Graff, etc.) you will probably make more money selling it to an estate jewelry buyer or gold buyer.

If you have real gold (and to a lesser degree silver) and the jewelry is broken, seriously out-of-style, not signed or not made by a desirable maker, you may want to sell the metal for scrap. Gold prices fluctuate but have been mostly on an upward trend. As of this writing, gold is trading at over $1,500 an ounce. (Whereas silver is a bit under $16 an ounce.) Google "today's gold price" or "spot gold price" to find out the going rates.

To turn gold into cash, you will generally go to a jeweler, a "we buy gold!" place or a pawn shop that buys gold. Do not use one of the online gold buyers (even if you see them on TV!), as they have a very high swindlers-to-legit-buyers ratio.

That said, while possibly not the least scammy industry out there, there are certainly gold-buyers who are perfectly pleasant and reputable business people and a little vetting will help you find them. If you live in a place big enough to have multiple gold-selling options within a reasonable distance, you'll want to do some research before deciding who to approach:

- Check out reviews on Yelp or your favorite review site

- Ask for personal recommendations

- Look at the websites of your various options to help determine their credibility and suitability

- Call in advance and ask what percentage they give for scrap gold (and silver)[5]

---

5 Scrap dealers do not give you the full daily rate for your metal, as they need to make a profit on it themselves, as well charging for their services of brokering it to the next stage in the melt-resell-reuse process. I'd be interested in anyone giving at least 80%... and the higher above that the better.

Is it real gold?

- The easiest clue is a gold mark. Look for markings like 10K, 14K, 18K, 22K or 24K. This is most common system in the US and Canada You may want to whip out your handy magnifying glass for this task. A lighted jeweler's loupe is about $10 online and is incredibly handy in this situation. (Like this one: **amzn.to/33tsAiM**)

- Different countries mark their gold in different ways. See the chart below for some other numbers that are equivalent to the purity measures used in the US and Canada.

- If your piece is antique, it may be real but not have any marks.

- Try a neodymium magnet on the piece (stronger than most fridge magnets). If the jewelry is magnetic, it's not gold (or silver or platinum). (Like this one: **amzn.to/2NvKD2s**)

- Pieces from Europe will usually have a country mark (a crown, an animal, something heraldic, etc.) along with the purity mark. They'll usually also have a maker's mark.

- Pieces from the UK use a fairly complicated system of hallmarks which can tell you a lot once deciphered, including where and when a piece was made. For your secret decoder ring, poke around the Birmingham Assay Office website. Start here: **bit.ly/assayoffice**

- If you get really into this, you can buy a pretty easy-to-use gold- and silver- testing kit online for less than $10. (Like this: **amzn. to/2qEePiA**)

- You can also bring your stuff to a jeweler or place that buys gold/silver and have them test it for you. They should give you a quote without the obligation to sell it to them.

Is it *not* gold?

- Gold-filled jewelry is usually marked "GF" or often "GF" plus a fractional number which equates to the small amount of gold purity present. It's essentially just metal coated with a very thin veneer of gold. Older pieces (pre-1980s) may actually have the gold rubbed off in places, which is an easy tell for gold plate.

- If you find "Pd", that's palladium. "PT" is platinum. "SS" is stainless steel. "CZ" means any stones present are cubic zirconia.

- False gold marks are possible. Not common, but possible. If you see a number that isn't in the "Gold Numbers" chart below, become suspicious and test with a backup method.

Gold Numbers

This table shows you the karat and purity percentage equivalencies of the number you might find stamped on your gold.

STAMP	PURITY
375	9 karat (37.5%)
585	14 karat (58.5%)
750	18 karat (75.0%)
916	22 karat (91.6%)

Gold value

There are two ways to turn gold into usable cash money: sell it in the form it's in or sell it to be melted.

- If your piece is antique, a brand name, well-designed, or if it has real gold/platinum/stones it may well be worth more as a piece of jewelry than for melt value. Consult a jeweler.

- If you have broken jewelry, single earrings, or pieces of questionable aesthetic value (especially anything grievously out of style which would be a hard sell as is), you might want to investigate its melt value.

  » When you see the quoted daily spot price for gold, it's for "pure", 24K gold. You probably don't have that. You more likely have 10K, 14K, 18K, or 22K. Each of these karat amounts describes a piece's percentage of pure gold measured in 24ths, of all things. (The remaining content is an alloy of another metal.) Thus, 18K gold is 75% pure and 14K gold is 58.3% pure.

  » 10K is only 41.7% gold and is generally not considered "fine jewelry". 10K may still be worth selling if you have a lot of it, but it won't bring much.

» You can use math to determine the value of a piece. It's the percentage of pure gold *times* the gold spot price *times* the weight in the same unit of measurement as the spot price. Or you can use one of the online calculators. Try: **goldcalc.com.** Jewelers use a very exact scale to weigh metals, but you if you already have a digital food or postal scale, these can give you a very reasonable approximation of how much metal you have. You should know this going in to any possible buying deal so you can tell if you're getting a fair price. (Or, buy a cheap scale like this: **amzn.to/2Ocv9j4**)

» If there are stones or watch faces/clockworks in your jewelry, you can just guestimate what percentage of the overall weight they comprise and subtract it to get the approximate gold weight.

» Gold-filled jewelry is rarely worth selling. If you have literal pounds of it, or a lot of older pieces (which often have a thicker plating), go for it. Some jewelers don't want to bother with gold-filled, but it never hurts to ask. Some will buy small quantities from you but you'll essentially get pennies for it. The cost of refining it to get the gold out often exceeds the value of the gold.

» If the stones are very large or you're feeling particularly exacting, you can Google up an array of mathematical formulas to aid you in your precision. Try **bit.ly/ goldestimate.**

» When you bring your pile of gold in to the jeweler, they may tell you the weight in grams, troy ounces, grains, or regular ounces. If they are nice and reputable and not trying to pull a fast one, they'll convert that unit of measurement to one with which you're more familiar if you ask. But, if you want to come prepared, you can weigh your gold and then use one of many online calculators to convert the weight to the other types of measurements. Try: **bit.ly/goldunit**

• You don't have to take what a buyer offers you. You can also go to multiple buyers and see who makes the best offer before deciding whom to sell to. A way to be less awkward about this exercise is to use the little white lie: "I'm required by the estate to get three prices and take the highest".

- Tell the jeweler to let you know if there are pieces that would be more valuable to sell as they are than to melt. If they are honest, they'll help you with this whether or not they are in the market to buy intact jewelry.

A word about silver

Silver has an array of possible markings as well. The easiest one is pretty common, it will say STERLING. This is what you want. A few of the others:

- Mexican silver may say MEXICO SILVER or have any number of marks (check some out here: **bit.ly/mexsilver**)

- Silver can be marked by purity with a few different systems. See the "Silver Numbers" chart below for equivalencies.

Silver numbers

STAMP	PURITY
800	80% pure silver
925	92.5% pure silver
968	96.8 pure silver
999	99.9% pure silver

Silver value

Silver being worth so much less than gold in melt value, you'll have to make a gut call as to whether what you have will sell for more intact or as scrap (remember that you're only likely to get 80-90% of the spot price from a good scrap buyer). So if a piece of jewelry has any aesthetic merit or any possible appeal at all, you might want to try selling it as is instead of scrapping it.

On the other hand, if you have big pieces of sterling such as serving pieces or sets of flatware, bowls, candlesticks are other decorative items, scrapping may be a decent prospect. You'll want to make sure these pieces are STERLING rather than silverplate, which is not usually worth much beyond its aesthetic value. You can use the same gold/silver testing kit I mentioned before for this (**amzn.to/2qEePiA**) or ask a jeweler to do a test for you.

For the most part, today's younger generations aren't interested in owning silver flatware (or fine china and crystal), so these items can be a hard sell. A big, solid sterling serving spoon could, however, bring you $60 or $70 in scrap value. A big bowl could be in the hundreds. If your tableware is not of historical or major aesthetic significance and/or made by a known luxury brand name maker you might want to melt it.

Non-precious Metals

Metals, such as copper, brass, aluminum, zinc, iron, and steel can also be scrapped for money. The prices you'll get for them are exponentially lower than what precious metals command. For various reasons, there could be a lot of scrappable metal at the estate you're selling, such as:

- An electrician, plumber, contractor, etc. lived there and brought home their work
- A hoarding situation with an industrial bent
- A demolition sale

The easiest approach to a situation like this is to include the scrap metal details when you advertise your sale. There are people who scrap regularly (and in bulk) and who will find it worth their time to come and collect your metal (even if it means unscrewing wrought iron porch railings or what-have-you). Give them a good price to encourage them to come clear up for you.

If selling your metal at the sale doesn't work, you can try offering it just after the sale (on Craigslist, for example) for a very low price or free if someone will cart it all away.

For an approach that will maximize your profits, you can research local scrapyards and either bring in the metal yourself or see if they will come pick it up (not out of the question).

Google "scrap prices today" to get an idea how much different materials are worth per pound. Though scrap metal is not likely your path to fortune, it is a lot more ecologically responsible to scrap (aka recycle) rather than sending it to a landfill directly.

Fashion and vintage Costume Jewelry

Vintage costume jewelry can actually do pretty well at estate sales, but for the most part you'll make money on quantity rather than high prices per piece. People are attracted to shiny objects and may buy jewelry on impulse if it isn't too expensive.

As of 2020, vintage jewelry made up until the end of the 1960s is the most collected. People will also buy jewelry from the 1970s up until the present, usually for everyday wear, not collectible reasons. Certain kinds of pieces can be desirable no matter when they were made.

To see what you've got, you should first check to see if you have pieces with a marker's mark on them — or what is called "signed" costume jewelry. Some signed pieces can be surprisingly valuable and sought-after.

Here is a list of just a few brands which are well-collected:

- Weiss
- Eisenberg
- Hobe
- Coro or Corocraft
- Lisner
- Napier
- Trifari
- Boucher
- Miriam Haskell
- Carnegie
- Florenza
- Kramer
- Sarah Coventry
- Van Dell
- Whiting & Davis
- Bogoff
- MMA (Metropolitan Museum of Art)

There are zillions more makers who signed their jewelry than I've listed above. A great place to research them is this directory: **bit.ly/ signedcostume**

If you find a mark, you'll want to look up what similar pieces have sold for in the past. The best way to do this is to look at online reselling sites, such as eBay and Etsy. The section "Definitely, possibly, or perhaps a wee-bit
special items" on page 35 provides much greater detail on doing pricing research, but here are a few basics:

Etsy
On Etsy (**etsy.com**) look at the prices at which similar pieces are listed to give you a ballpark idea of value. How people have listed items here can also help you figure out what, exactly, you have. Remember, these list prices are what someone has decided to try to sell the piece for, not a price at which they have demonstrably sold in the past. It may or may not accurately reflect what the market will pay.

eBay
On eBay (**eBay.com**) you can search on the maker's name, the type of jewelry, and then choose the filter to show only *sold items*. Sort these results from highest price to lowest. This will give you an idea of the range in which these kinds of items sell.

Selling options
If you find that you have a potentially valuable piece of costume jewelry, or enough somewhat valuable pieces that you might want to pursue selling them before/outside of the sale, here are a few options:

- You can try selling the items on eBay. The advantage here is that you should be able to sell them at the going rate. The disadvantage is that they might sit for a long time before selling. Also, listing on eBay requires more effort than selling in your sale.
  - » You'll want to take very good photographs — including close-ups — preferably on a white background. You should make sure to show as much detail as possible including the maker's mark. You should be able to take these photos with your cell phone camera as long as you have some bright, even lighting. You can use natural light or a lamp positioned on each side of the

piece. For a backdrop, try a big sheet of clean white paper that curves up behind the subject.

» Make sure you put the words (keywords) in the title on your listing that people would be searching for. At a minimum, use the maker's name and the kind of jewelry.

» Put your listing in the appropriate category on eBay by copying what other sellers did with similar items.

» There are lots of pricing strategies on eBay but I would recommend pricing somewhat high compared to similar items and using the "Best Offer" option. This will allow buyers to make offers which you can choose to accept or counter. This is often a good way to psychologically plant the idea and your buyers' minds that the piece is valuable and that they're getting a deal by offering you less than you've asked for.

» Be aware that there are some fees associated with selling on eBay including a possible listing fee, final value fee, and PayPal fee. You will also have to decide whether the buyer pays for shipping or whether you'll cover it — and whether or not you're willing to ship internationally.

- Sell your pieces to an antique store, or to another dealer of vintage jewelry. Bear in mind that you will get a price that allows the store to make a profit when they sell the piece on. The advantage here is getting rid of a lot of fiddly small items at once and guaranteeing yourself probably around 50% of retail value for them.

- Consign your pieces to a live auction. Generally, you'll leave pieces with the auction house and after the sale (which you can attend if you like), they'll pay you for anything that sold and return anything that didn't. They'll take a cut of the sales price, of course.

Auctions

There are a bunch of kinds of live auctions in the world, but for the purposes of this book I'll be talking about two different kinds:

1. National, International, or Specialist auctions: these are what I think of as the "big guys". These are the auction houses you may have heard of, like Christies or Sothby's. These will sometimes be appropriate venues for selling truly valuable items. The "specialist auctions" I refer to in this category are when, for example, Christies does an "Indian Sculpture Auction" or a "Fine Watches" auction. I wouldn't even start to consider going this route for anything worth less than $5,000.

2. Local live auctions: whether you've ever stumbled across them or not, there are probably auctioneers that run events near you. These can vary from summer "barn sales" to higher end affairs with art and antiques. Many are in between. These auction houses often buy out estates and sell them off and/or they take consignments big and small from dealers (or everyday people) and split the proceeds if the items sell. A lot of these "local" auctions have a very low barrier to entry for selling your stuff, whatever it is. To locate some auctions (and thus auctioneers) near you try: **auctionzip.com**

Some **live auctions also simulcast on the web these days, increasing their audience and potential bidders to a global scale.**

Watches

Traditional watches are pretty much on the outs these days. Another item for which the youth doesn't find much use. Luxury brands (Patek Philippe, Rolex, Tag Heuer, Cartier, Omega, Montblanc, etc.) will still sell for good money, but the majority of watches — even antique pocket watches — are usually worth less than you might guess. Rather than bothering with any special treatment, you'll probably just want to sell most in your estate sale.

That said, it's worth doing a little research on any watches, as there can be pricey outliers in any lot of $10 plain janes. You should also check for gold or silver markings. You can sell a watch bezel or band or pocket watch case for scrap like anything else.

Google around to find out how to tell what model and year your watch is. Each brand has different little tricks for finding the serial number and the date of manufacture. If you have the original box, papers, receipt, or any other paraphernalia that came with a watch, this will add to its value.

You can get an idea of what your watch is worth by checking out listings for similar items that have sold on eBay or on specialist online watch-reselling sites.

If you happen to have a luxury or highly collectible watch to sell, it's definitely worth running it by a jeweler or dealer to see if they will buy it, or doing a little research and then trying to sell it yourself on eBay or a watch-specific reselling site.

If you have a *really* valuable watch (worth more than $5,000 or so) it may be worth your while to contact some higher end auction houses for a (usually free) appraisal and possible entry into a specialist watch sale. This will be advertised to, and attended by, watch people. You'll have the potential to make a good return (even though the auction house will take a cut). Try Sotheby's, Christie's, Antiquorum, or Bonhams.

Collectibles

The collectibles universe is wide and deep. Although different kinds of collections can be sold through different means, there are a few common approaches you can take.

Collectibles can do well at an estate sale, especially the kinds of collectibles that appeal to a lot of people and that sell in a low-medium price range. I think of these as the kind of collectibles that you might display in a bookcase, not the kind you'd keep in locked glass cabinet or safe. In fact, these kinds of items can do a great job to help you market your sale — lots of people will come *because* of the collectibles. And they can encourage people to come early with cash in hand, fearing they'll miss out.

This list is by no means exhaustive, but here are some of the types of collectibles I'm talking about:

- Figurines and decorative collectibles
- Toys and games
- Clocks
- Glassware

- China
- Sports cards and memorabilia
- Non-sports trading cards (Star Wars cards, Garbage Pail kids, etc.) or role-playing game cards (Magic the Gathering, Pokémon, etc.)
- Christmas/Holiday decorations
- Cookie Jars
- Dolls and stuffed animals
- Comic books
- Your aunt's collection of turtle knickknacks or your dad's hoard of golf-joke-themed sweaters
- Fine writing instruments (fountain pens, etc.)
- Models and kits
- Action figures
- Sci-fi and horror collectibles
- Entertainment collectibles
- Coins and stamps
- Barware, liquor, and beer collectibles
- Military items
- Knives
- Ephemera
- Railroadiana (i.e. train stuff, model trains)
- Photographs and postcards
- Coke, Pepsi, Disney, etc. items
- Vintage textiles or clothes
- Old video games, consoles, and accessories
- Old computers (especially Apple, Commodore, Atari, etc.)
- Old books
- Music (records, CDs, etc.)
- Old magazines or significant newspapers
- Tobacco collectibles
- Any other collection around a topic

In any one of these kinds of collection, you may have one or more item that *is* actually safety-deposit-box worthy, and if this is the case, you may choose to sell it in a more specialized way.

If you have collectibles which are "slabbed and graded" (comics, sports cards, coins, etc.) or otherwise officially appraised and documented (dolls, action figures, etc.), you should be able to figure out their current market value with a little internet research. Then, you may want to offer them to the appropriate specialist dealer or, if valuable enough, put them in a specialist auction. (Try: **ha.com**) A dealer will give you less than retail and an auction will take a cut, but both have the potential to get you more for your rare (or rare-ish) item than you'll get at an estate sale. Both have the ability to reach the particular collectors who are more likely to pay up for that special something.

Similarly, you can consider selling cohesive collections (stamps, old books, knives, ephemera, etc.) of low to medium value to a dealer or consigning with a local live auction. If you can't find a specialist dealer or auction, usually a generalist one will also suffice. Think about the likelihood of someone buying your dad's collection of 40 albums of not-very-individually-valuable postage stamps at the sale versus a dealer buying them at an auction of all sorts of "estate stuff". The latter is often more likely.

If you do choose to sell all your collectibles at the sale, including any particularly valuable ones, make sure to implement appropriate measures to keep the items safe until they sell (see "Security" on page 28).

Art

Art is fairly straightforward. If you have pieces, in any medium, (painting, sculpture, original prints or photographs, etc.) that are signed by a known artist or that you believe to be valuable for whatever reason, you should probably get them appraised. (By the way, the artist doesn't have to be "known" by you — look them up online and see what you find.)

For pieces you suspect may be worth some money (several thousand or more) your best bet is to inquire with one of the big auction houses. Often you can fill out an online form and they'll tell you if they want to see more and do a free appraisal. If they can tell from your online form that it's not going to be worth their time, they'll let you know and that will give you a clue about the price as well. You can try the big guys — Sotheby's, Christie's, Bonhams, etc.— for pieces that seem significant. For art more in the $100-1000 value range, Google up your local art auctioneers).

Art that is not by known artists, however great it is, is usually considered to be more of "decorative" value. You can try placing pieces in a local live generalist auction, but you might as well just sell it at your sale, to minimize effort.

Clothing and accessories

For the most part, you'll just want to sell clothing, shoes, purses, belts and the like at your sale. However, there are a few possible exceptions you may want to consider.

- Any **Haute Couture** (bespoke designer) items you'll probably want to try to sell for a higher price to a specialist.

- **Luxury designer clothes, handbags, or accessories** (Gucci, Hermès, Prada, etc.). For these items you can try to sell to a dealer, at a specialist auction or consign either online or in person. There are several online sites that deal in luxury authentication and consignment. Try The Real Real (therealreal.com), ThredUp Luxe (thredup.com/luxe), or Vestaire Collective (us.vestiairecollective.com) — be sure to read their current consignment terms and payout structure). In general, for luxury items, you'll get at least 40% (sometimes a lot more) of what the piece sells for and all you have to do is mail it to the selling platform company. They market to an interested audience you might not get at your sale and do all the important authentication and photography work for you.

- **Vintage clothing.** If you have clothing from the 1970s or earlier you may want to look into selling it at a specialist vintage clothing auction or dealer — especially in these subcategories:
  - » Any couture
  - » Any historically significant designer (Dior, Chanel, Saint Laurent, etc.)
  - » Collections or pieces that are iconic to their period (70s maxi dresses, 60s mod dresses, 50s poodle skirts and twin sets, 40s New Look dresses, 30s bias cut dresses)
  - » Any clothes from the 20s or earlier. Victorian,

Edwardian, Flapper. All sought after.

  » Jeans. Vintage Levi's from as recently as the 90s are very desirable. Jeans older than that (Levi's and other brands) can be quite valuable. Grandpa's old ripped up work pants from the 40s could be like gold.

- **Furs.** You may or may not get someone at your sale who wants Aunt Patty's mink. And you're not likely to get a ton of cash for it. While a vintage fur coat might have cost $5,000 new, at best it might sell for $250 at an antique store today, and you'd be lucky to get $75 for it at an estate sale. Furs are not easy to move. You may just go for it and sell it for whatever you get, but if you're feeling more ambitious, there are online platforms that specifically buy furs. (Try **buymyfur.com, cashforfurcoats.com** or **vintage-furs.com**). You can also try eBay for furs, though that will likely take much longer. In my experience, furs do not do well at live auctions.

- **Other clothes.**

  » **Baby and kids clothes.** These will almost definitely sell well at your estate sale if you advertise that you have them. They won't bring in a mint, but they should go. If you want to experiment, you can also try selling them on your local Facebook mum's groups or to a local kids' consignment shop. The money will likely be fairly similar with all of these options, however.

  » **The rest.** Everything else you should try to sell at your sale first and then, possibly reassess what doesn't sell. Individually selling or consigning your general everyday clothes and accessories (even if they're "nice") takes a lot of effort and usually doesn't have a huge return.

Weapons

If you have guns, firearms or a significant amount of ammunition to dispose of, check the laws for your country, state, and/or province, and city, as they vary widely. Carefully consider whether or not you want to sell a gun privately, thus allowing the new owner not to leave the weapon registered to your name and then pursue potentially nefarious intentions. For local gun laws in the US, try: **nraila.org**

Regardless of profit comparisons, you may choose, categorically, to sell any guns or knives, bows or other weapons to a dealer or at a specialist auction to decrease safety and liability issues and to help assure a sale to a new owner who has been vetted (if you locality requires it).

You can also turn in guns, ammo, or other weapons to the local police department if you'd rather get them off the streets completely.

Assessing the space

Think about the space in which you'll hold your sale and make some mental or actual notes. The sections that follow will give you food for thought.

Bathrooms

Bathrooms are almost never available for shoppers at estate sales. Sometimes this is because the water has been shut off in the property, but more often it's just to prevent mess, shoplifting, and whatever shenanigans "the public" might think to get up to in private.

Think about whether you want to use the bathrooms to store not-for-sale items or sale supplies like extra boxes and packing materials.

By the way, if a person seems desperate enough, and bold enough to ask, and the toilet is in working order, feel free to use your discretion and let them go.

Blocked off areas

Are there spaces that are full of items which will not be in the sale? It may be easier to bring out anything you *will* sell and then block those spaces off. The same goes for closets or cupboards. You can even block off sections of rooms or cover not-for-sale piles with sheets.

Estate sales often allow shoppers into basements, garages, and attics — in fact these are many shoppers' favorite spots at sales — so don't forget to make decisions about these areas.

High-risk areas

When professionals estate sale companies run sales, they do so knowing that they carry liability insurance in case someone goes through that hole in the attic floor or trips into that pile of old chainsaws in the basement. While, hopefully there is still homeowners' insurance in place that will cover suits from such situations (see "Insurance" on page 43), and more hopefully, nothing untoward will happen anyway, you should make some decisions about whether you want to let people into any more dangerous or hard-to-access spaces.

If you plan to close off your stuff-packed, awkward attic or beastly basement, you will want to figure out if it's possible to remove their sellable contents to a more accessible area. If that's going to be a horrible or logistically impossible task, you might want to consider advertising on craigslist for someone to buy the contents in their entirety with caveats that they take full responsibility for removing the items from the precarious situation. Or you might just decide to let people in there at the sale after all. I've been to lots of estate sales where you can climb or crawl into all sorts of crazy spaces (at your own risk). Just use your best judgement and your personal risk-tolerance meter.

You can help people out with a liberal sprinkling of "watch your step/ head" signs, and neon tape on the steps of the weirdly steep staircase.

Security

Believe it or not, people do shoplift at estate sales. Not everyone, not always, but it can happen. If you're dealing with a large or nook-prolific space, you might consider closing off areas to cut down on the number of people you will need to have around to adequately patrol these spaces.

Or, you might not feel like bothering to be stressed out about a small degree of potential petty larceny, which is also a legitimate position.

What you will want to do is find a way to concentrate items which are both small(ish) and valuable(ish) in an area that will be monitored — but we'll discuss that further as we go.

Traffic flow

In and out

Choose one door for people to come in and go out during the sale. This could be a front, back, or side door, a garage door, a patio slider, what-have-you. Just narrow it down to one. This will make your job much easier in terms of crowd control, cashing people out, and security.

Cashier

Organized sales always have a cashier located near the entrance/exit. This person sometimes helps orient people when they enter, but their main job is to check people out. They handle the money and recordkeeping. Think about where you can place some sort of table or desk near the exit. While you're at it, determine if there's some sort of folding table, desk, kitchen counter, board and saw horses or other flat-surface-like contraption amongst the sale items that you can appropriate for the cashier's domain. Ideally, this will be something you're planning on trashing (a totally messed up card table you can throw a blanket over for the sale). If it's something you might viably sell, don't forget to let people know that with signage.

Routes

It's not necessary that you micromanage how people navigate your sale, but think about how shoppers might move through the space and where you might need to help them find more rooms to explore. Think about rooms they might miss if they enter and exit through the door you've designated.

Floors

Consciously choose a level of prophylactic floor protection. Here are common techniques:

- Whatever. The floors are all hardwood and you can sweep and mop once everything's out. It's all good.

- Door mat, umbrella stand, "please wipe your feet" sign. Self-explanatory.

- Roll up rugs, even if they're for sale, and let people unroll to view as needed.

- Ask people at the door to either take their shoes off or don protective booties — the ones that are common in museums or for surgeons. (try: amzn.to/37M5qG1).

Display surfaces

There are estate sales where everything is everywhere willy-nilly. This can be a valid technique if you're dealing with a hoarder-type situation or a premises that's otherwise pretty much a disaster. In fact, these types of sales attract a certain kind of adventurous shopper. If the property you're dealing with is like this, you can skip this section.

If, however, you can or want to put in some elbow grease to maximize the visibility and desirability of what you're selling, do some assessment of what spaces you have for display, such as:

- Built-in shelves or cabinets
- Furniture (bureaus, beds, shelves, cabinets, desks, tables, etc.)
- Counters and bars
- Pegboards or built in racks
- Closets

Also consider what you have that can help you use empty/floor space as display space.

- Bins and totes
- Boxes and large storage containers
- Stands
- Makeshift shelves (cinder blocks and boards)
- Makeshift tables (door or boards propped on saw horses or file cabinets, etc.)
- Clothes racks
- Over the door racks or hooks

Are there already hooks or nails in the walls you can use to display art and/or hang cloth items? Can you bang some in without consequence (i.e., the property will be painted before sale, or is slated for renovation or demolition)?

You can use hangers to hook items (blankets, linens, sleeping bags, clothes, etc.) over doors or on handles to cabinets not in use for the sale. You can string some rope as a clothesline type display.

If you're really stretched for hanging space for art or anything else you could buy some removable hooks (try: amzn.to/35B9J5I) or borrow or rent some clothing racks.

Small, valuable and/or breakable

Make sure to consider what areas and techniques will be best for displaying small, valuable and/or breakable items. Some common techniques:

- Generally, concentrate this stuff near the cashier. People will be more careful and less shoplift-y if under surveillance.

- Display small/valuable items like jewelry (real or costume) on the cashier table if there's room

- Display breakable items in a china cabinet or other cabinet with glass doors

- Display less-breakable but still fancy/valuable items higher up and more breakable items more at eye-level and lower (with the theory that it's easier to pick something up that you can see and reach well, and that the least fragile things have the furthest to fall)

- Display very fragile and/or valuable items in closed glass front cabinet or other visible but hard-to-access area with signage saying "please ask to see the _____"

Part Two: Researching prices

Even if you eventually choose not to use price tags, or to use them only sparsely, you'll want to research prices for any items that may hold value so you know what to charge people (or where to begin negotiations). Usually, these items to research will be in the arts and collectibles realm. So, unless you already know the score, you'll want to research any:

- Art
- Antiques
- Jewelry (real or costume)
- Pottery, fancy glassware, barware, dishware, etc.
- Fancy nicknacks
- Vintage collectibles (entertainment memorabilia, advertising, toys, games, etc.)
- Designer anything (clothes, shoes, bags, jewelry, perfume, nicknacks, etc.)
- Old or collectible books, records, media in other formats
- Anything weird, old, expensive-when-purchased-originally, or that you don't know how to price

---

Definitions

Vintage is considered 20 years old or more, while **antique** is considered 100 years old or more.

Prices at an estate sale should be lower than you'd find the same items in a retail store, antique store, gallery, boutique, high-end auctions, or even on eBay. This is a venue where people expect bargains to one degree or another, and they're not going to pay full price. You're also likely to get some shoppers who are actually resellers, looking for items to flip in their own stores or online — and they're not going to bite unless they see a viable profit margin.

The nothing special items (aka, the easy stuff)

First off, there are probably tons of items you can price by instinct, by lot, and/or by category. Here's the technique:

> Say there's a kitchen full of run-of-the-mill utensils (spatulas, slotted spoons, can openers, turkey basters, etc.). Just pick a single price that will apply to any one of them. Somewhere between 25¢ and $2 a piece is likely to be appropriate. Choose your price based on the general quality of items, tenor of the sale, and your goals. Group them in one place, (or don't), and stick up a sign in the general area that says, "Kitchen Utensils $1/a piece". When people are checking out, you should use this price as the starting point if they want to negotiate, or for giving them a bulk deal if they're buying a lot.

You can use the same strategy for other kinds of items too, with the caveat that you should pull out and separately price any special or more valuable items within the given groupings:

- Sets of everyday glassware, dishware, cutlery, flowerpots, and the like

- Kitchen, bath, garage, and cleaning consumables (dish soap, shampoo, aluminum foil, potting soil)[6]

- Books (you can graduate the prices for paperbacks, magazines, children's books, hardcovers, coffee table books, etc. if you want). Books can be a hard sale, so go lower rather than higher. X for $X deals (i.e. 3 for $5) can be an effective technique.

- Media (DVDs, CDs, records, computer games, console games)

---

6 This is an insider reseller secret: If you find any health and beauty or household products that you know are not made anymore, or that are old or odd, look them up on eBay and Amazon. In-demand discontinued products can sell for surprising premiums. We're talking $50-100 for an old bottle of shampoo or a carpet cleaner that someone is obsessed with but can no longer buy in stores. If you find one of these peculiar gems, you might want to list it on eBay if you can, and wait for a buyer.

- Like kinds of toys (action figures, stuffed animals, board games, puzzles)
- Clothing or shoes
- Like-ish kinds of crafting, sewing, art or office supplies
- Cables, cords, wires, powerstrips etc.
- You get the idea…

Most of the items above will also be priced in the 25¢–$2 a piece realm (using the US dollar in the 2020 economy). Clothing and shoes may land more in $2–$5 price range in most cases — but remember, where talking about the nothing-special items here. You'll be pulling out the things that should be priced higher.

Definitely, possibly, or perhaps a wee-bit special items

For anything that you know or think may go for a bit more, you have two choices: wing it or research it.

If you wing it, you may be "leaving money on the table" but it will be fast and easy and people will be pleased with the deals they're getting.

If you decide to research, you'll feel more confident in your prices and will maximize your take. And, you will learn as you research, giving you a gut feel for how to price similar items and speed up your work.

Comparables (aka comps)

In the same way that a realtor will price a house based on prices for similar houses in the area, you can use comps to give you an idea how to price your items.

Usually, eBay will be your first stop for comps. Here's how to work it:

1. Go to **eBay.com**
2. Type a description of the item in the search box
3. When your results come up, click the "sold items" filter
4. Now look at the results

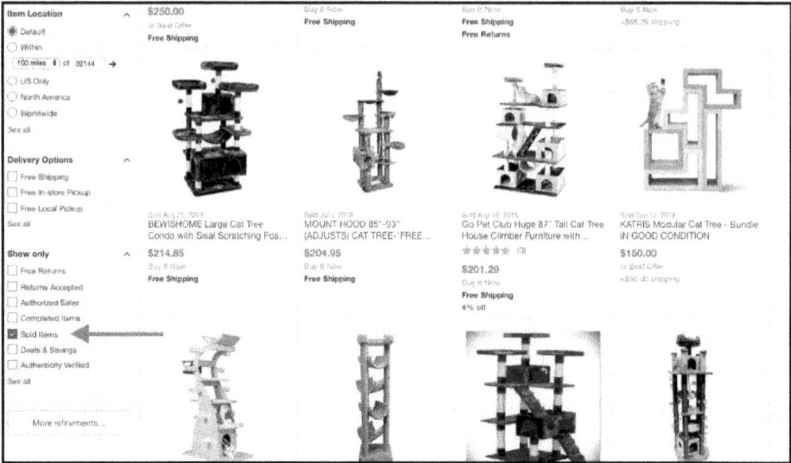
The "Sold Items" filter on eBay

Note: in the mobile app, the "Sold" filter is found in the hamburger pop up menu

You can now sort these results from highest to lowest price, or narrow in on items more like what you have by using filters or more descriptive words in your search terms.

In the biz, we call this "looking at solds" (ok, at least that's what I call it). It is crucial that you're researching what the item *sold for* rather than what it's *listed for*. The former is a relatively accurate indicator of what the second hand market will bear in terms of pricing for that item. The latter is some arbitrary price that some random person chooses to stick an item on eBay for. Indeed, it is a price at which no one has chosen to purchase said item, as of yet.

---

eBay printouts

Nothing galls a seasoned estate-sale goer more than seeing printouts from eBay with *list prices* taped to an item to rationalize an unrealistic asking price. Don't do it! Don't print out the sold prices either. Keep this info under your hat, my friend.

Analyzing solds

If you find an item exactly or reasonably-enough like yours and all the prices are around the same, you're golden. Based on your goals, gut feel, and the style of your sale, price you item somewhere between 50-100% of what it's going for on eBay.

If you find a range of prices, use an average or your best judgment and then apply the 50-100% idea. Remember to look for items that are in a similar condition to yours.

If you find only one or just a few similar items and they went for a seemingly freakishly low price, check to see if they sold as an auction. If so, click through to the full listing page and click the link that says the number of bids. It currently looks like this:

Bidding has ended on this item.

FENTON VASELINE OPALESCENT HOBNAIL RUFFLED CANDY DISH (PRE LOGO) See original listing

Condition:	Used
Ended:	Aug 03, 2019 , 1:13PM
Winning bid:	US $17.50 [4 bids] ⟵
Shipping:	$9.50 Economy Shipping
Item location:	Port Saint Lucie, Florida, United States
Seller:	lampnutz (5388 ☆) ｜ Seller's other items

Sell one like this

The link on an eBay sold item page which takes you to the bidding history

When you follow this link, you'll see a bidding history. You'll be able to see what price the lister started the item at. Note if the set starting bid was low (i.e. 99¢) and how many bidders there were.

The way the eBay auction system works, buyers enter their maximum bid, or the most they'd be willing to pay for the item. With each bid the eBay algorithm only increases the going price by a small, predetermined increment. regardless of bidders' maximum prices. This way, the person who has bid the most, at the time the auction ends, becomes the winner, but they're price is only X (eBay's incrementor) times the number of bidders. Because of this, auctions with a low number of bidders don't necessarily reflect the real market rate for an item.

Here's an example "Bid history" from a vintage costume jewelry donkey pin:

This seller listed the item at 99¢ and put it up for auction. Apparently, the demand for donkey pins wasn't exploding on 9 August 2019 at 6:15am. This item only got one bid, so it stayed at the initial asking price and the buyer got it for 99¢. But is this a fair example of what a vintage Coro donkey pin goes for? Maybe, maybe not.

Here's another Coro donkey pin. This time it was listed at a set price (not an auction) of $9.99. It then sold for $9.99. Is this a fair market value for a Coro donkey pin? Maybe... it's more informative for us than the 99¢ auction was. It tells us that someone, somewhere, would pay at least $9.99.

But would they pay more if the seller had priced it higher? That, we don't really know. One way to gauge it is to uncheck the Sold filter and see if any are listed, but as yet unpurchased.

And yup, today, there are two:

Vintage Coro Textured Gold Tone Donkey
Pin Brooch Political Democrat
$10.19 Was: $11.99
Buy It Now
+$3.90 shipping
15% off
♡ Watch

Vintage Coro Donkey Rhinestone eye
brooch-Co223
$25.00
Buy It Now
+$5.66 shipping
♡ Watch

Someone has one listed for just a bit more than the one that sold for $9.99, at $10.19. But they have it on sale, down from $11.99 (note the crossed-out price and the "15% off"). This could mean no one was biting at $11.99 and they're trying to move it. As yet, no one is biting at $10.19, either.

Then there's another one, listed at $25. Perhaps this person is in it for the long game, and they'll wait until there are no cheaper donkeys available and that just-right person comes along who'll pay $25. But it's an outlier to be sure.

After analyzing this research, if I were selling a Coro donkey pin like this at my sale, I'd probably price it at $5. I think that's even a little optimistic for a small, unflashy item like this in the context of an estate sale. But it gives you room to negotiate. I can see pricing it at $6 if there wasn't a lot of costume jewelry and this item would stand out. I can see pricing it at $1-2 if it was one amongst many shinier, more interesting jewelry items.

Now, all this is not to say that I recommend putting exhaustive research into a $5 donkey pin. It's just an example of the principle. You might turn up the same kind of information for a $500 Chinese vase.

More places to do research

What if you can't find your item on eBay? You could base your pricing on reasonably similar items you do find (like a Coro elephant pin). Or you can expand your research.

Start by doing a Google search for your item and then flipping to the "Images" tab to help you locate it (or something similar) more quickly.

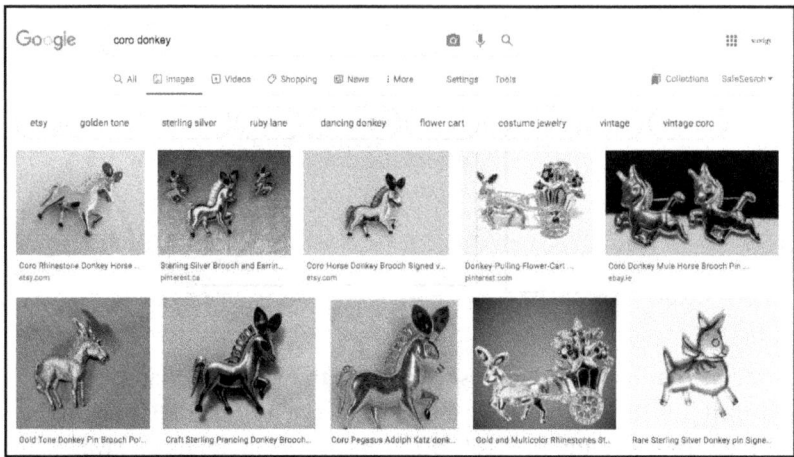

Google Images search results

Click through to any leads and see if they include pricing information (noting how old the information is).

Through Google Images, you may find vintage items listed on etsy. While etsy doesn't show "solds", I tend to find that etsy list pricing reflects market value better than eBay. Why, I don't know. Perhaps because etsy sellers are more diligent price researchers, or, because there are relatively fewer listings on Etsy, there is less variation apparent. At any rate, take it with a grain of salt, but look at what etsy people think the item is worth to give you some ideas.

You may find links to one of the millions of no-name-recognition small sites selling things online, especially vintage, antique or collectible items. Again, if you're lucky, there will be some pricing, and you can, after analyzing the context in which it's being priced, use it as a gauge for your item.

You may also stumble upon a paid price guide site. Some of the big ones are **worthpoint.com** and **kovels.com**. Here you'll be frustrated to find some details of your item are shown but that you are restricted from seeing the price information. On **Kovels.com** you can sign up for a free account and see price records. On **worthpoint.com**, you can sign up for a rather wimpy free trial that (as of the moment) allows you 7 days of access or 7 lookups. This won't get you too far, but might be useful if you're dying of curiosity about a price record and are good at canceling free trials before your credit card gets billed.

If you aren't getting good enough info from eBay or the big price guide sites, try googling the item type plus "price guide".

Alternately, you can also spend some time at a library or bookstore looking at physical price guide books. Big bookstores usually have sections with books that cover a lot of different categories of antiques and collectibles. With these, bear in mind that the "book values" are inevitably out-of-date and generally run very high vs. market value.

Part Three: Getting Ready

Ducks to get in a row

Insurance

Bearing in mind that I'm neither an insurance professional nor a lawyer, here's a few thoughts about insurance. In an ideal situation, there'd be liability and slip and fall insurance for the property you're working at. In the real world, there may be extant homeowners insurance *if you're lucky*.

If you're especially risk-averse, you might want to call your insurance agent and ask for advice. Otherwise, consider this a one-time event and put reasonable precautions in place in how you set up the sale, make sure to include liability-waiving verbiage in your advertising, and don't worry about it.

Timing

When to have your sale will probably be dictated by a lot of external factors somewhat beyond your control. There may be legalities, or you may need to sell the house in short order. Or, you may actually have a life and need to get this over with.

If you have a choice, here are some factors to consider when setting a date:

- Choose a time with the best chance of pleasant weather in your location
- Give yourself as much advanced time to get ready as you need
- Choose a weekend if at all possible

Duration

From my non-statistically significant observations, I'd say estate sales are most commonly held over 2-3 days. But you can configure your sale as needed. Here are some arrangements I've seen, roughly ranked from most to least common:

- 2 days: Saturday and Sunday
- 2 days: Friday and Saturday
- 3 days: Friday-Sunday
- 1 day: Saturday
- 1 day: Sunday
- 1 day: weekday
- Every weekend or every Saturday until the stuff is gone

Hours

By tradition, estate sales, like yard sales, start early in the morning: 8 or 9am. You can choose to accept or reject this tradition. Your sale can start whenever you want it to.

Along with the early starts, people tend to wind up between 3 and 5pm each day, and you can do this if you see fit — or not. Sometimes people make the first or last day a short day... perhaps not opening until Friday afternoon or ending with a Sunday 9-12 stint.

You can also advertise times but then stay open later if it's busy and people keep coming. Or close early (leave a sign) if it's ridiculously slow. Your choice.

Finally, you may choose to advertise your sale only for one day (Saturday, say) and then extend it for a second day (Sunday, or even the next Saturday). This can be a good tactic if you have the flexibility and haven't sold as much as you'd like, especially if the weather has conspired to give you a poor turn out.

Ads

Advertising your sale is, not surprisingly, extremely important. You can do all manner of guerilla marketing, but I'd strongly advise placing ads online in at least two places if you're in the US:

- **Estatesales.net** (costs money)
- **Craigslist.org** (free)

You might also want to advertise in your local paper, church/synagogue/mosque bulletin or any other physical or electronic publication with a short lead time and that local folks actually use to find out about events. You can also put up flyers on telephone poles and bulletin boards or bring a stack to an event that permits it. But neither of these is as important as hitting up the two key online spots.

If you're in Canada, you should list your sale on of **craigslist.org**, **kijiji.ca**, and/or your local Facebook marketplace — which ever ones are used most commonly in your area.

Estatesales.net

This is the go-to spot for regular estate sale shoppers in the US. As of this writing, it costs $79 to advertise here, but you should get a good return on investment with the increased number of attendees.

Making your estatesales.net ad: detailed instructions

- Go to the site and choose "List a Sale".
- Use the "private listing" option — that means that you're a one-time estate sale organizer, not an estate company which advertises sales regularly. It doesn't mean that your sale or ad are "private" in any way.

Name

For the name of your sale choose something informative and interesting or unique. Check out how some other sales are listed by typing in your zip code on the estatesales.net homepage. Lots of them have very generic names like "Houston Estate Sale" or "Huge Estate Sale". The town location shows up in your listing automatically, so don't waste your title space with that. Try something more along the lines of:

- Car collectors dream! 1918 Packard, auto toys & advertising
- Luxuries abound! Designer bags and shoes in high-end estate
- Large mid-century home filled to the brim with furniture and art
- Tools, collectibles, housewares, tons of books and kids' stuff

If your sale is high-end... i.e., a nice house in a nice neighborhood with expensive things, indicate or imply that in your title with keywords like:

- Luxury
- Designer
- Expensive taste
- Curated collection
- Exquisite, elegant, etc.

If your sale property is stuffed, cluttered, hoarded, or otherwise quite full, you can clue in certain kinds of buyers with words like:

- Picker's paradise, picker's dream, picker heaven, etc.[7]
- Treasure hunt, Antique hunt, Collectibles hunt, etc.
- Packed, packed door to door, packed floor to ceiling, stuffed, loaded, etc.

Title length

Only about 68-70 characters show up for title field for viewers using a computer. Less for those using mobile phones. Check to make sure yours isn't too cut off and make sure to "front load" some of the most important words. You can use a site like **lettercount.com** to help you with your crafting.

Details
Fill in all the easy details: location, dates, time and so forth. Note that the site will automatically hide the exact address until the day before the sale, only showing the town until then. This is for your protection — against burglaries, harassment and the like.

Terms and Conditions
Here's where you put your rules and policies for the sale so people know what to expect. This may or may not hold up as a legal disclaimer in a court of law, but it certainly can't hurt.

You can format it however you like, but here are some details to make sure to include in the Terms and Conditions (T&C) section:

---

7 I apologize that the word "picker" is kind of a gross. But, in "the biz" it's shorthand for people who sort through the chaff for the treasure... especially the crazy messy chaff.

- What form(s) of payment you accept
- Whether or not you'll provide help for people to carry things out
- Whether or not you'll supply boxes, bags, and/or packing materials
- That all sales are final
- Parking directions
- That you're not responsible for accidents
- Whether or not everything purchased must be removed the day(s) of the sale
- Whether or not you offer delivery
- Early birds policy
- Weather cancellation policy

A great way to get ideas about content and wording for this T&C section is to look at what the professional estate sale companies do in current listings. On top of that, here's an example of what your T&C might look like (feel free to take out or add in items):

- We accept cash and credit cards (no checks).
- Bring help to carry out large items.
- We have some boxes and packing material, but bring your own to be safe.
- All items are sold "as is" and all sales are final.
- We are not responsible for accidents.
- We are on a small road but parking is allowed on the west side. Observe any no parking signs. Please show respect for our neighbors and do not block driveways.
- We prefer that all items be removed during the sale, but you may arrange for pickup on Monday if necessary.
- We do not offer delivery but there is a Home Depot 3 blocks away where a small truck may be rented on an hourly basis.
- No early birds will be admitted to the sale. Please do not line up before 7am. If you arrive before doors open, you may start a list, which we will honor at 9am. Anyone on the list who is not

present loses their place.

- In case of snow, we will post an update here as to whether or not the sale will go on.

Early birds

People like to catch the proverbial estate sale worm, and to that end, will sometimes line up at ridiculously early hours to guarantee they get into a sale amongst the first people. Especially promising sales have been known to attract lines of people as early as the night before.

The tradition, or etiquette for all this is that someone (either a person waiting, or a person from the sale) starts a numbered list of those in line early and, when doors open, they are admitted in that order. Sometimes there are rules about not leaving the line once you're in it — or having someone hold your place, yea or nay. Most of the time (but not always), people are adults about the situation and let others go and come back if they need coffee or the bathroom. At larger sales with anticipated crowds of early birds (say, an antique store being liquidated, or something exciting like that), a representative from the sale team will hand out numbers to people waiting and keep an eye on the crowd. This probably will not be the case with your sale, but you never know.

Description

You can write as much or as little as you want in this section, but I find that the more successful descriptions make the sale sound appealing and friendly, give you a sense of its character, and also list relevant specifics.

Again, check out what the professional estate sale companies are putting in their description sections and notice what kinds of info and format makes you want to go to their sales.

I think the best formula is to be informative but not so wordy that people can't be bothered to plow through your description. Try:

- 1-3 sentence intro that gives the character of the sale and generates a sense of excitement
- An easy-to-scan list of specific item highlights
- A friendly closing

This might end up something like:

> Packed sale in Smithwood! Family home of 40 years filled with collectibles, craft supplies, dolls, antique and French country furniture and lots more.
>
> Highlights include:
> - Large collection of German bisque dolls
> - Victorian horsehair settee, gorgeously restored and reupholstered
> - Tons of scrapbooking supplies, rubber stamps, paints, paper, stickers, albums, & more
> - Ralph Lauren living room furniture and linens
> - Old books, games, toys, and children's items
> - Vintage radios
> - [and then list some more stuff]
>
> We look forward to seeing you Saturday or Sunday!

Of course, put your own spin on it. Add in anything that you think buyers should know. Just keep it straightforward and cleanly formatted.

Photos
As of this writing, you are allowed to include up to 50 photos for the price of your ad and you can add additional ones for more money. Don't pay for more unless you can justify the extra photos with extra income you think will be made by having them.

Do, however use all 50 free photo slots. You can also put captions on each photo, which most people don't bother with — but feel free, it will enhance the information you're providing.

Taking photos
First of all, don't let this stress you out. You don't have to be a professional and you don't have to have a fancy camera. A cell phone camera or whatever digital you can get your hands on is perfectly fine. Your strategy for taking pictures should be:

- Make sure to get individual or small group shots of your best items

- Make the majority of your photos "portraits" of specific items rather than views of rooms or areas — you want viewers to be able to focus on something or some things in each photos rather than just get a sense of overwhelm. A few room, area, or tableau shots are fine though. They give a sense of the sale's character and breadth.

- Feel free to take closeup photos of designer labels, pottery marks and the like if those are a feature of your sale

- Even if you haven't finished (or even started!) staging yet, fake it and place things where you need them to show them off

- Good lighting is really important: you don't need to set up anything special, but open the blinds, turn on the lights, make the environment bright. This will help immensely with capturing details and getting non-blurry photos. If your photos are blurry or dark, try to:

  » wait for a day where there's more sun

  » move items to a brighter area if possible

  » brace your camera on something (anything — a tripod, a table, your arm) to keep it more still

  » grab a lamp from somewhere to light the area

  » turn on your camera's image stabilization feature, if it has one

  » make sure your autofocus setting is on and that it's adjusting fully before taking the shot

- Don't get too caught up about composition or any technical photography stuff. These photographs are ephemeral and informational. Just keep each shot as clear and simple as you can.

Here are some examples of aesthetically unexceptional but perfectly acceptable estate sale ad photos:

That's about it for your estatesales.net ad. Placing it three weeks prior to your sale is optimal (you can update it whenever you're ready with more photos and details). Two weeks is good, one week will do in a pinch.

Craigslist

This will be easier. Take all the text you wrote and pictures you took for estatesales.net and plop 'em in a Craigslist ad for your area under the "Garage Sale" category. Put your description first, then your T&C. At the beginning, end, or both, write some text saying that the address for the sale will be posted the day before it happens (and for now, just include the town).

Remember to update your ad with the address the day before your sale.

If you are outside the US, please adapt the directions above to suit your local popular listing sites.

Helpers

You'll want to have some helpers for your sale if possible. With any luck you can recruit friends and family who'll help for free (or for a free lunch). If not, you can try paying some young people you might know a small wage, or, in an absolute pinch hire someone from a temporary placement services like **taskrabbit.com** or **thumbtack.com**.

There are a bunch of roles which need to be filled at an estate sale, but you can be creative with combining them if you have a smaller "staff" in place. I've certainly been to sales run by one or two people by themselves, and things have gone fine. Many more professional sales have quite a few people, perhaps one for each room of the house, but being in "the biz" and working for clients, means these companies have a more serious concern about shoplifting and more stake in quick set ups and clean-ups. Just get as many people as you can conveniently arrange.

Some of the jobs that need doing at estate sale on the day are:

Pricer
This is the final arbiter of what a customer pays. There are, however, a lot of variations on how this job can work (see below). The important part is that they are the one person who has the final say/authority.

Cashier
Obviously, this is the money handler. They cash people out, make change and send them on their way.

Greeter
It's nice to have someone welcoming people to the sale and telling folks what rooms are open and some general sale info.

Security
You may want to have someone keeping an eye on what's going on in various rooms, areas, or floors of the house. This can be more or less important depending on the type of sale. For very large sales or ones with small, expensive items everywhere, you'll probably want to pay attention to this role. For sales where you've got tons of lower-priced

stuff and you'd be glad of whatever you can get any money for, you can be a bit more laissez-faire. A lot depends on your attitude towards the issue as well. People *do* sometimes pocket items at estate sales — not all the time, and not everybody, but it does happen.

Gopher/General Helper/Restager

Having someone around who can do whatever the person-in-charge needs is a great bonus. You may have them rustle up boxes or bags for shoppers, grab items someone is asking about, show people to the kinds of merchandise they're interested in, or help people carry things out to their cars (if you want to offer that). They can also help to move items from hidden areas (cabinets, etc.) to more obvious areas as things sell and room frees up (see "Re-staging as you go" on page 76).

The jobs of Greeter, Security, Gopher, General Helper, and Restager can be combined into one person or split arbitrarily amongst everyone available.

Pricer techniques

In reality, the Pricer and Cashier are often one in the same person, with one or two other people doing everything else.

If the Pricer and Cashier *are* the same person, they don't need to stay stationary at the checkout table ("Traffic flow" on page 29). A system like this will probably work better:

- Everyone working the sale knows to send all shoppers to the Pricer/Cashier to get prices and/or check out

- A sign near the door tells people: "Find Sophia when you're ready to check out. She has a name tag".

- Sophia wears an obvious name tag, and circulates, helping people with pricing, answering questions, and carrying the cash with her.

If the Pricer and Cashier are *different* people, you can still make the pricing person obvious with the name tag schtick, but the Pricer sends the buyer off to the Cashier after they talk. The Pricer can give the buyer a slip or paper or receipt book page with the agreed-upon price to bring to the cashier. Often, in this situation, the Cashier will have a sign at their table saying, "Cashier cannot change prices". This keeps the price arbitration and haggling confined to the one person in charge.

Similarly, if all items are priced with tags and signs and haggling is either off the table or left to anyone on the team's discretion, everyone working the sale can be equipped with a receipt book or notepad and can price items for buyers. In big, popular sales there is sometimes a person in each room or on each floor tallying up what people have gathered as they move through the sale (and then they bring their slip, with notes from the different room-minders, to the cashier at the end to be tallied and paid.) This method is partially a security and smooth-workflow measure, but it also plays the psychological trick on buyers of making them feel committed to buying what they've picked up along the way rather than culling down their shopping basket with a more curating eye towards the end of their shopping.

Supplies

There are a bunch of simple tools of the trade that you'll want to pick up to help everything go smoothly. Feel free to improvise where you're inspired to.

Signs

- Posterboard
- Big marker
- Duct tape (for outside signs)
- Blue painter's tape (for inside signs)
- Regular or colored paper (8.5x11")

Figure out how many signs you'll need for your sale. You'll want:

- One *on* the house
- One or more on the road in front of the house (more if there's a long driveway or confusing approach
- Two (one facing each way) for the turn(s) onto the street the house is on
- More for further afield, to direct traffic to the street and house, as needed

Posterboard. Usually the half-size posterboard, used vertically (about 14x22") works best for fitting on telephone poles and street signs while still being reasonably large. I like to get all one color, instead of a variety, so as to create predictable visual consistency when someone is following the signs in their car. This will be cheaper if you buy it locally at a store than if you buy it online, but you're looking for something like this: **amzn.to/35gLERR**

Marker. Any bold black one will do. Go bolder than a conventional Sharpie if you can (the Sharpie King Size or Sharpie Magnum are good). You want to create a sign people can catch the gist of from their car. Find a marker something like this: **amzn.to/2qsXtFU**

Duct tape. In terms of tape you don't need duct tape, *per se,* but you'll likely find the stickiness (or lack thereof) of clear packing tape frustrating when trying to affix signs to telephone poles and the like.

Painter's tape. The painters' tape (and regular paper) is for putting up signs inside the house. The painters' tape won't damage the walls and is easy to remove. Of course, if that's not an issue, use Scotch, duct, masking, or whatever you have on hand.

Money

Shortly before the sale, pop into a bank and get $100-200 in varied bills and some change.

You can get a cash box from an office supply store if you're feeling fancy, but it's probably overkill for a one-time sale. Another small box (something like a cigar box) or even some envelopes or small accordion folder would work. In a pinch, a wad of cash in your pocket or a fanny pack/bum bag is also fine.

Digital Money Options

As of this writing, there are a boatload of competing ways you can collect money using credit cards or electronic payments using a cellphone with or without an add-on card reader. They're all pretty easy to deal with, and it's worth using one (or more), as it encourages people to spend more if they don't have to have the cash on them. You will, however, want to set them up (and test them) ahead of time. Though there are many more than these, I'd recommend:

- Square (**squareup.com**)
- PayPal (**paypal.com**)
- Venmo (**venmo.com**)

Each works a little differently, so check out their websites and see what suits you best.

Checks
Whether or not you choose to accept personal and/or business checks is up to you. I've seen sales go both ways.

Receipts

If you have to or want to keep track of what sells, and for how much in any sort of granular way, you might want to pick up one or more sales order books with carbonless copies, like this one: **amzn.to/35y9J6A**.

If you have a single person pricing, they can write up an itemized receipt for each person who makes purchases. The Pricer will keep the carbon copy of the receipt for the records and give the original to the shopper, who will bring it to the Cashier (if this is a different person than the Pricer) to show what they owe.

If you have multiple people pricing (in different rooms, for example), they can each wield a receipt book and give shoppers itemized slips. All the carbon copies in all the receipt books can be compiled at the end of the sale and considered the official record.

Alternately, you can also just keep a running money tally at the cashier desk and not worry about the details, or simply count the money at the end of the day and subtract the change you started with.

Price stickers

If you're going to use price stickers (we'll talk more about this choice later), the packs of round or rectangular stickers from the office supply store (like this: **amzn.to/2tEMhHq**) are fine. If you have some of these lying around, make sure they're still sticky enough to stay on for a while. I've noticed those things get unsticky when they're old and leave you with annoying puddles of price stickers on the floor and unpriced items.

You can also opt for some blue painter's tape or masking tape and a permanent marker to make stickers.

Bags, boxes, wrapping supplies

People like to grab a bag to collect their treasures in while perusing the sale or a bag or box to carry their purchases out in. If you happen to have bags or boxes on hand (destined for recycling or saved for reuse), it's a nice amenity to give them out while they last.

By the same token, if you have newspaper, bubble wrap or anything else that can be used to wrap fragile items, it's good to get that together and stash it near the checkout.

This stuff is optional — don't spend money to buy it — but if you happen to have some already, put it to use.

Creative reuse

Some houses accumulate collections of things that aren't quite worth selling but may be useful in the sales process.

- Old towels, shop rags, or linens that aren't desirable enough to sell but aren't gross can be used for wrapping delicate purchases
- Miscellaneous office or craft paper can be used for wrapping or to make signs
- Plastic bins or totes or other organizing containers can be used to sort and display items (but use signs to make clear that they're also for sale).
- Reusable shopping bags (or saved paper/plastic ones) can be given out to shoppers for carrying out their purchases.

Sorting, staging, and price-tagging

The next big tasks in front of you are sorting, staging, and price-tagging. You can do these in a linear fashion, in just that order, but you also may wish to combine them. There's a lot to be said for the cleaning/organizing truism "touch each item only once" — and if you want to stick to that ideal, you'll sort, stage, and price each item rather than doing a full sort, a full stage, and then pricing.

You'll probably end up doing something of an amalgamation of the two methods — because often you need the *context* of the full complement of like items to know where to put something, how to arrange groups of things, and to determine what their relative prices are.

Sorting strategy

How much you choose to sort will depend on the condition of the house to begin with and how much time and effort you have to put in to the sale. Here are some examples of the end results of sorting seen pretty regularly:

- **Total hoarder house:** no sorting what-so-ever. At the sale itself, everything is everywhere, on the floor, in boxes, on every surface, completely random mêlée.

- **Controlled chaos:** nothing is sorted very granularly, but there is some semblance of order. At the sale, people will find some, but not too much stuff on the floor surrounded by cluttered rooms and surfaces — but at least looks like someone could have lived there.

- **Sensibly sorted:** Most items have been identified and returned to the room in which they belong (i.e., cookware in the kitchen, clothes in the bedroom). Like items are put together to some degree — perhaps women's clothes together, men's clothes together, books together, office supplies together, computer gadgets together, etc. Some areas, like the basement, attic, or garage may be fairly tumultuous.

- **Store-level merchandizing:** everything sorted into like items in relevant rooms, displays of products placed purposefully, bins or boxes holding collections of like loose objects, etc.

More on these sorting styles

Total hoarder house

In a situation where the house is in a bad state (perhaps it's not been lived in for a while, was left a bit trashed, or was the residence of someone with hoarding tendencies), you may choose not to sort at all. It's wise to review what you have as best you can so you can do any necessary advanced research about pricing. You'll also want to remove dangerous items to the best of your ability. If there's black mold in the bathroom, a hole in the attic floor, thousands of rats in basement, etc. you'll want to just block those areas off to the public (and yourself).

For example, I went to a sale in my own neighborhood once and was nosy-neighbor shocked to enter the 3-storey house and discover that it was a hoarder maelstrom. The living room, where the people running the sale were checking people out, had some space to move, but the rest of the property from basement to attic was at least a foot deep in stuff with no order to it what-so-ever. I don't know what the story was, exactly, or how it got quite so bad. I would guess an elderly person lived there and died with no one in the family wanting to take responsibility for the estate. The wallpaper, remaining décor and appliances were solidly 1960s or earlier and the neglect had progressed to the point where there was caution tape around some holes in the floor. The people running this sale pulled out anything valuable and sent it to auction, then they left everything else as is.

Controlled chaos
If you have an excessive amount of stuff for the space but it's not completely preposterous, you may want to focus on rescuing and showcasing the more potentially valuable, fragile (or desirably shop-liftable) pieces and leave the rest more or less as is.

For example, I attended a sale once where a man seemed to be selling off his wife or mother's huge collection of medium- to high-end clothes. I don't know how they all were stored in the small split-level house before the sale (seems like it would defy physics!) but all he did was get about 20 clothing racks and fill every room with hanging clothes. There were also random boxes and laundry baskets on the floors all over the place filled with shirts and sweaters and shoes and purses. It was not organized… like things were not together and it was messy — but shoppers could go through the racks of clothes systematically and enjoy the thrill of the hunt. This sale also sported a basement room that was pretty organized and a garage that was a chaos of Christmas stuff, old luggage, tools and bits of furniture stuffed with sundries. For this man, he was going to make the money of his sale selling the designer and other nice clothes, and I think his focus on making them accessible in an otherwise messy environment was a good choice.

Sensibly sorted
Most sales fall in this territory, and it's probably a reasonable place to aim for on the effort-to-fanciness-to-overkill spectrum.

These sales can vary greatly in appearance but generally look like a "normal" house that people lived in to some degree — be it very stripped down or very filled up.

For the "sensible sort" methodology, gauge the amount of time which is practical for you to work on this (realizing it's probably going to take a lot longer than you're estimating), consider the state of the house as it is, and then decide what's most important to arrange before the sale.

If the house is already fairly tidy and organized, you don't have much to do except, again, pull out the potentially valuable, fragile or desirably shop-liftable pieces for more surveilled display and perhaps showcase other interesting or sought-after items.

You may just work on big picture sorting, or you may get pretty gung-ho and arrange everything quite nicely. How far you go is all just a matter of time and effort. If you want to take it to the next level and really group and display items to their best advantage, go for it.

Store-level merchandizing
Some shoppers love a truly organized, glamorous sale. Most don't really pay much attention and are fine with any degree of "sensibly sorted". Some shoppers (myself included) also love the thrill of the treasure hunt in a thoroughly disordered house... and especially its grimy basement and attic. That's all to say that, unless you're really enjoying yourself, I wouldn't bother to go as far as making each table at your estate sale look like a Macy's Christmas window display.

General staging tactics and aesthetics
Here is a general rule for displaying items:

>**The more obvious and in the line of sight something is, the more likely it is to sell.**

Only a portion of shoppers will poke into drawers and cabinets or look in nooks and crannies. Only a portion of shoppers will look things over carefully at all. So, the more things you can make clearly visible without shoppers having to exert effort, the better.

If you have too much to have everything out, consider leaving cabinets open and drawers partially open. You can put also put signs on cabinets, closets, and drawers that say, "Open Me!".

You don't need to reinvent the wheel when setting up displays. Books can stay in bookcases or on shelves. Clothes can hang in closets (though you may want to pull out select special items to display with hangers on doors or elsewhere where they'll catch the eye). Use flat surfaces to spread out and display items which normally hide in day-to-day life. Display as much out in the open as possible — even if it means a stack of board games on top of an office filing cabinet or a collection of usually garage-bound Christmas ornaments on the dining room table.

Christmas

People love Christmas and will buy it all year round, so don't be shy with wrapping paper, holiday table wear, collectibles, and even fake Christmas trees — no matter how balmy the June weather. (Also true for Halloween, Hunukah, Passover, and Easter).

Put the nice (expensive) things that have a good chance of selling in the most prominent places. The same goes for any weird items that people might not otherwise consider — weird stuff gets people talking and more engaged if nothing else.

If there are dark areas in some rooms, see if you can move lamps from other areas to brighten them up or spotlight items that are easy to pass by. Open the shades or curtains to let as much light in as possible.

If you have insurmountably dark places (such as basements or attics), consider having some flashlights for people to borrow. Scrounge them from the sale or your own home if you can — I wouldn't invest money in new flashlights. Most people have lights on their phone these days (though you may have to remind them of this).

If a space is truly dark and treacherous, but you want to let people go there anyway, Put up a sign saying something like "Attic has no lights and uneven floorboards — Enter at your own risk"

Sorting and staging timeframe

To help make yourself a sorting schedule and set yourself some expectations, note how long a discrete chunk (a room, for example) takes to organize and then multiply it by the number of similar chunks there are. In other words, if it takes you 4 hours to sort an averagely chaotic room, and there are 6 rooms total, then the whole sort will take you about 24 hours of time.

Actually doing the sorting

Once you've decided on your approximate goals for sorting, let the games begin!

Start moving things about to get them into the right rooms. Start grouping like items in bins or baskets or on tables, or in whatever manner makes sense.

Remove, or sequester in blocked-off areas, any items that should not be in the sale as you come across them.

There's not a lot to wax on about when it comes to the actual sorting. It's a brute force activity you just have to power through. Personally, I'm the 8-hours-on-a-Sunday type, but you may choose to work in smaller chunks as time allows.

Window treatments

If the window treatments are for sale, put some signs near the to say so. It's completely all right to give the person wants to buy them a step stool and a screwdriver and make them uninstall what they want. Same goes for cabinet knobs, switch plates, doorknobs or anything else attached to the house that is ok for you to sell.

The other setup logistics

Along with sorting and staging items, there are some other tasks on your setting-up list.

Off-limits areas

- Decide what rooms (if any) will not be used in the sale. Make "No Entry" signs and affix them to those rooms' doors with painter's tape.
    » Block off any cabinets, drawers, or shelves similarly with "Do not open" or "Not for Sale" signs as needed.
    » Use tape (or string, or police tape, or yarn, or whatever you have) to block off entire areas as needed: half of a room, a portion of an open space, a room with no door.

> » Close bathroom doors and put "No Entry" signs on them.

- Label any pieces of furniture, appliances or other large/unmovable items "Not for sale".

Old-fashioned manners

Add a "please" to all your signs to give your sale a friendly feel. You'd be surprised how rarely this is done!

Entry and Checkout

Your goal is to have a single point of entry and exit for your shoppers. This helps control numbers, keeps checkout orderly and limits shoplifting opportunities.

Choose a door that will be as easy to get in and out of as possible. Many older properties were not designed with the needs of people with disabilities or ambulatory difficulties in mind, but if you can use an entrance without stairs or tricky footing, do so.

Once you've determined your entrance/exit, give all the other ways in and out the "do not enter" treatment.

Think about where your checkout table will be relative to the exit/entrance. Generally, it's best to have it nearby the door but off to the side enough that you're not impeding anyone's path. Some ideas:

- Set up your checkout station *outside* the entry/exit door if the climate makes it feasible.
- Set it up in the doorway to a room that is not being used in the sale, and let the cashier become a *de facto* barricade.
- Use an alcove or foyer area where there's not much shopping to be done anyway.
- Use a room off to the side of the entry/exit door and place the checkout station in the middle of a large room (or against a wall in a smaller room) to allow people to shop around the cashier

When you've figured out where you want to put your checkout station, set up some sort of table or desk there. This can be anything, really: a card or folding table, a desk, a kitchen breakfast bar (if handily placed) or, an old door on some saw horses.

If it seems to need it, you might want to cover your table with a table cloth (i.e., a sheet, blanket, actual tablecloth, whatever you have kicking around). This gives you a nicer look and lets you hide stuff underneath the table.

Requisition a chair or stool from the sale for your check out person to sit on (but don't decline to sell it out from under them if you get a good offer!)

If your checkout table is commodious enough, you can use it to set up your smaller, more valuable, and/or most shop-liftable items for sale. These tend to include:

- Jewelry and costume jewelry
- Small trinkets
- Coins, medals, pins, patches and the like
- Featured special items or collections (e.g., autographed photos, antique maps, stamp collections, camera equipment, a Fabergé egg...)

Also think about whether or not there are larger items which you'd like to keep an eye on. (An expensive and delicate statue, an antique chair that people shouldn't sit on, etc.) and consider placing these items within the eyelines of the checkout person.

The final (indoor) signs

To wrap up the logistical portion of staging, there a few more kinds of signs you may want or need to make and post.

Caution

If there are any places where shoppers should watch their step or take extra care, put up a sign. Remember, that even if you are familiar with the property and wouldn't think twice about that step down to the den, you'll be entertaining people who have never visited before and may have poor eyesight, walk with difficulty, or may be just generally unobservant. Common sites for caution signs include:

- A step up or down between rooms
- A low overhead on the way to a basement or attic (or low-hanging ceiling fan)
- Uneven floors or rugs that can trip people
- Narrow, steep, or otherwise rickety stairs

Wayfinding
These are the signs that will help people navigate and participate in the sale. Examples:

- More in Garage! This Way →
- Basement →
- Attic →
- More outside →
- More →
- Checkout →

Anywhere you're selling stuff that someone unfamiliar with the property might miss, stick a sign with an arrow.

Rules
You might also want some signs that explain how things work at your sale:

- Cash only
- We take credit cards over $10
- See anyone with an apron for pricing
- Cashier cannot negotiate prices

Overall price-tagging strategy

In general, how you decide to price will depend on your goals. If you want to move merch and clean house, low prices and giving people good deals will help. If you want or need to recoup as much as possible, higher prices with built-in negotiating room are the way you'll want to go.

If you're dealing with an upscale property with designer, luxury and high-end items, you'll want price everything on the higher end of the scale, with even the small items priced relatively higher than they might be elsewhere (though not exorbitant... you still want them to sell!)

If your property is more middle- to low-end, chaotic, overfull, full of discount store items, etc., you'll want to price everything according to a cheaper relative scale.

And, obviously, if it's in-between you'll likewise go for in-between prices.

Price tags and signs

Whether or not you actually put price tags on your merchandise is up to you. Here's a glimpse at the spectrum of price-tagging possibilities:

METHOD	PROS	CONS
Put price tags on everything. Use individual stickers on items and signs that give prices for categories of items (e.g., "Paperbacks 2/$1)	• You don't have to price on the fly • You have a no-brainer starting place to negotiate from with hagglers. • You will somewhat discourage haggling. • You'll make shy shoppers more comfortable. • Ability to use pricing strategies (see below).	• It's a ton of work. • You may discourage bulk-deal shoppers. • You'll possibly discourage non-haggling type shoppers if your prices are too high. • It might seem a little "control-freaky" to regular estate sale shoppers and resellers and put them off, especially if your stated prices are high.

METHOD	PROS	CONS
Put price tags on some items. Use category pricing signs for the cheap stuff to give shoppers a ballpark idea of what they'll expect to pay and give the impression that there are good deals at your sale (e.g. "All Tupperware 25¢"). Maybe price a few other key items that you know you want to get a certain amount for to discourage low-ballers (e.g. "Gucci bag $150 firm")	• It's not a huge amount of work. • You have less to price on the fly. • Shoppers love to dig out items to get a stated good deal (like that huge box of 25¢ Tupperware). • You'll help make shy shoppers more comfortable. • Ability to use pricing strategies (see below).	• People who are too shy to ask for prices may steer away from unpriced items. • Even if you put tags on items you want to get a certain amount for, some shoppers will still low-ball or haggle.
Don't use price tags at all.	• Quick and easy. • Don't have to obtain stickers or pricing supplies. • Allows you tons of latitude for negotiation and spontaneity based on the moment-to-moment "market" at your sale.	• Your prices, or even your ranges are a complete unknown to shoppers which may put them off. • Shy shoppers may be scared to make offers or inquire. • No ability to use pricing strategies (see below).

Pricing Strategies (aka tricks)

As a shopper in the world, you've no doubt noticed that retailers use some tricks to get you to buy, buy more or get interested. Here are some techniques and psychological strategies you can choose to employ if you like:

Price anchoring

The general concept of price anchoring is that you set a number for the item's value in the consumer's mind and then delight them by making the price they actually have to pay lower than that anchor.

The classic implementation, in traditional retail, is to show the "full price" on a tag but then offer the item for less, either through "slashing" that price and replacing it with a discount price on the tag, or through a sale that pertains to that item. Think discount retailers like TJMaxx.

There are lots of studies about anchoring, many showing a surprising amount of arbitrariness and latitude are possible in the first part — where you cause the consumer develops an anchor price for what they think the item is worth.

Here are some ways to use price anchoring in the context of an estate sale:

- Create a universal discount late in your sale. For example: 50% off everything on Day 2. Or after 3pm during a 1-day sale.

- If you have price tags, display items you want to move next to similar but more highly priced items to make them seem cheap in comparison.

- "Slash" prices (on signs or tags) on certain items after the sale has gone on for a while. Literally, lightly cross out the first price you marked and write on a lower one.[8]

---

8 You don't want to start out with "slashed" prices for a number of reasons. Firstly, you want give buyers a chance to pay full price if they're going to. Secondly, consumers will be suspicious of slashed prices at the beginning of a sale and it may engender mistrust or be confusing. Thirdly, in more official realms (like retail stores) this practice of marking up just to mark down is usually illegal, so you don't really want to go there.

Multiples pricing

This is a great technique for estate sales. The idea is to offer bundle pricing to encourage shoppers to buy more. Examples:

- Dresses $5/each, 5 for $20
- Kitchen utensils 3 for a $1
- Buy a pair of shoes, get the second for half off

Odd Pricing

You're no doubt aware that retailers commonly end their prices in 9 or 99 to trick consumers into rounding down rather than up. Seems silly, but it does work, psychologically, much as we'd each like to deny it.

In an estate sale environment, you want to stay away from the 99¢ version. It will seem too cheesy and obvious, and also create nightmares making change. However, you may be able to use some well-placed 9s to your advantage. Consider, for example, pricing an armchair at $39 instead of $40 or an antique barrister bookcase at $299 instead of $300.

Loss Leader

In retail, a loss leader is an item that a store choses to make little-to-no profit on in order to get customers through the door and/or interested in surrounding or related items. In brick and mortar stores, these are usually the items at the ends of aisles or otherwise prominently displayed.

You won't have "endcaps" at your estate sale, but you can take advantage of this technique in a few ways:

- Offer something free with purchase (or purchases above a certain dollar amount). At a sale I held in a house will a zillion plastic storage bins in the basement, we offered a free bin with any purchase over $5 and they went like hotcakes.

- Put some low-priced items near the entrance to attract attention. You can use a "free box" where you put junk that seems unsellable (people *will* take it) or a 25¢ or 50¢ bin. Get people rummaging and engaged on their way in or while they're waiting to check out.

Part Four: On the Day(s)

This section covers the final tasks you'll need to do on the day or days of the sale and discusses how to optimize your sale for various situations and contingencies. Hurrah! You're through the hardest part of the work!

Signs

Your online ads have revealed the address of your sale the day before. Now it's time to do everything you can to help people find it. Arm one of your helpers (or yourself) with duct tape, an optional staple gun, and your pile of signs. Put up the signs on and in front of the house first, to catch random drive-bys. Do the ends of the road next, then move further afield, posting signs on the important turns people will need to make off the main roads or from downtown (if it's reasonably nearby).

Make sure to note, in your head or elsewhere, where the signs are, as it is important etiquette to take them down after your sale is over.

Creature comforts

Make sure you have water and/or the caffeinated beverages of your choice on hand in plentiful supply for you and your helpers. It's going to be a long day. Snacks can be nice too.

And be sure to wear clothes that are going to be comfortable for the duration and which can get dirty.

Helpers

Next, set your helpers to their tasks. Save a few minutes before doors open to explain their specific tasks or go over the general tasks that need to be taken care of during the sale.

Showtime and flow control

At the appointed time, open the door and welcome your shoppers, if there are any waiting. If you've managed to accumulate a line, with or without a "list" (see ""Early birds" on page 48), decide if it's a reasonable number of people to let in at once or if it's more sensible to control the flow by letting them in in smaller groups with a bit of time elapsing between them.

Greet people, give them a little orientation and a smile. (Or have a helper do this.)

How to be

On the whole, act as friendly, chatty, and interested in people as you can. Make people feel comfortable, that you appreciate their business, and that you are happy to listen to their small talk. When appropriate, give shoppers extra info about an item they're looking at, such as its features or history.

You'd be surprised at how grouchy and unapproachable many (professional) estate sale runners can be. Being friendly and interested (though not necessarily a soft bargainer) you're going to have a much better and more pleasant sale.

Kinds of shoppers you might meet

Every sale is different, of course, and so much will depend on where you are and what you have. But here are a few types of shoppers you may encounter:

The Professional. This person is buying to resell. They may have a brick and mortar shop, sell online, or at flea markets. They will tend to know what many items are and what they are worth in their particular selling venue. And they'll want to pay significantly less than that. That said, these are not shoppers to dread. They will often purchase your "best" items if you give them a price they can work with. They may also pull odd (to you) items out of nooks and crannies and get excited about them while you'd never give them much thought. If they're savvy, they'll look for bulk deals, and they're likely to haggle. They'll usually be more experienced than you at haggling and at understanding the range of estate sale pricing, so do the best you can. However, if it seems like they want to take advantage of you or bully you into prices with which you don't feel comfortable, just say no. If they want an item that badly, it's bound to have value and be of interest to someone else as well.

The Collector. This shopper is there for something specific that they got wind of in your ads. They may come early and beeline to whatever it is. They may not look at anything else. They are probably quite knowledgeable about this type of item and have a preconceived notion of what they want to pay for it. As with any other shopper, use your best judgment when balancing making a sale versus making big bucks. Don't let them intimidate you if you think they're trying to grab something for a steal. In a pinch, you can tell them a wee white lie and say you have to consult with [insert likely person here] and that you'll hold the item for them while you do that. Ask them to come back in 10 or 15 minutes and then go surreptitiously do some double checking of pricing on the internet on your phone.

The Hard Bargainer. Again, know that you'll probably get some of these types and try to psych yourself up to not be intimidated by them, if that's likely. If you like bargaining, great! If not, below for some tips.

The Stockpiler. A lot of people at a sale like to "make a pile". It might be in a bag or box they carry around with them and it might just be a heap near the checkout area. These are good customers, since they're buying a lot of items. Just make sure, even if they try to obfuscate matters in one way or another, that you know what they're taking and charge them a reasonable price.

The Inspector. If you happen to notice someone examining an item very closely or coming back to an item over and over, you likely have a good sale once they make the decision that the item meets their standards. Definitely try for a higher price if it's unmarked or full price if it has a sticker.

The Endless Shopper. These are people that seem to stay at your sale for hours and hours, or all day, or come back every day. It's fine, they're often good customers. They just want to make sure they see everything, or they have trouble with decision-making. As long as they're not acting suspicious, just let them be.

The Casual Shopper. On the other end of the spectrum, there will be people who pop in, get a general sense and then leave. Or they look in a couple rooms and buy a few little things. Again, don't worry about it, but save your most solicitous helpfulness for the higher rollers.

The Nosy Neighbor. Inevitably, you'll get folks from the neighborhood who are curious to see inside the house. Just letting you know.

Haggling even if you hate it

I completely understand if the idea of bargaining over prices has you in a tizzy — or at least feeling less than comfortable. The bad news is, that even if you put up signs everywhere that say "Prices Non-Negotiable" (which is a bad idea, by the way), you'll still get people making offers and wanting to haggle. The good news is that there are some tips that can help make it less painful, or at least less of an unknown:

- If you know someone who really *likes* haggling, see if you can get them to come and help.

- For any item for which getting a certain return is a concern, mark it up a little so you have wiggle room to come down

- Similarly, decide on a price you won't go below for cheapie stuff. Maybe it's only 50¢ or 25¢ or 10¢ — but try to recoup at least that much. This will give you a good basis for pricing large bulk lots, even if you're guesstimating.

- When a customer approaches you with an item, know, or immediately decide, what the lowest price you'll take for it is. Don't go below that.

- Be strong with pushy people but friendly with shy people. In other words, if a seasoned negotiator is playing hardball with you, match their tone as much as your personality will allow. If you give an inch, they'll take a mile. On the other hand, if a hesitant negotiator approaches you and you sense that giving them a deal will make the sale, couch your conversation in softer terms. Make specific offers to them — they'll probably accept. Ease any rejection of their suggestions with an apologetic tone and firm counteroffer.

- Don't let lowball offers offend you. People have different bargaining philosophies and may come from aggressive bargaining cultures. If someone offers you $5 on an item you have marked $50, just give a friendly laugh and bring the discussion back to the $40-50 range as many times as you need to. They may try to make it hard for you by getting a little passive-aggressive or giving you a guilt trip, but eventually they'll either cave in or give up. If you're getting worn down and really want to make the sale, you can use your judgment in accepting a price somewhere in the middle (but try not to do it just because you want to end the conversation — there are some really persistent hagglers out there!).

- Like lowballers, some hagglers come equipped with tactical complaints to try to get you to lower your price. Here are some examples:

> » I can get this for $x at such-and-such a place.
>
> » Can you give me a discount because this item is damaged?
>
> » This is totally overpriced. It isn't worth anything like that.
>
> » I've collected these thingamabobs for 20 years and they never go for more than $x.
>
> » This just garbage.
>
> » I only have $x.

- Here are some replies you can try (while not taking it personally and replying with a jovial air):

> » We need to get $x for that, sorry.
>
> » It's still early, if you come back at the end of the sale and it's still available, I'll be able to give you a better price.
>
> » I knew about the damage and priced accordingly. I still need to get $x for that.
>
> » If you can get it for $x at such-and-such a place, maybe you should go there, because I really can't go below $y. Sorry.
>
> » $x is the best I can do. (Implied: take it or leave it).
>
> » Sorry, $x is too low. How about $z? (Knowing they'll then offer and you'll accept $y).
>
> » If you leave your contact info I can let you know if it's still available at the end of the sale.
>
> » Make that wince-y pain face when someone makes an overly low offer, as if you couldn't help such a reaction to such a ridiculous offer.
>
> » The nearest ATM is at the corner on the left.

» I really can't go that low... honestly I'd rather donate this to someone who needs it and get a tax deduction.

» You don't have to buy it.

Re-staging as you go

As items sell and prime display real estate opens up, fill it with articles that were previously more buried. If you have helpers, this is a great task for them to stay vigilant about. This can be especially useful in areas like the kitchen where objects sitting on the counter will attract more attention than those inside cabinets or drawers.

Price strategy as the sale goes on

Professional estate sale companies usually implement a universal discount at the end of a sale. This could be on day 3 of 3, in the afternoon of day 2 of 2 or even in the last hour or two of a one day sale. The discount can be as low as 25% off, but it's usually 50% — or just generally letting it be known that "we're making good deals now!".

You can announce the discount plan ahead of time (usually on the day of), or make it a spontaneous occurrence, letting word spread through the sale at the time it happens. For a multi-day sale, you can even add it to your ad the night before.

If you announce ahead of time what and when the discount will be, people may show up especially for the discounts. You may also have some shoppers who pile up stuff and then linger until after the clock strikes the magic discount hour before checking out, but that's not usually a huge concern.

If you play it by ear, you can start the heavy discounts when you feel like the time is right — stuff isn't moving any more, you have too much left and it's making you nervous, or you're exhausted and want to end a little earlier.

Take down signs

Your last task, after the sale closes on its final day, is to go take down the signs you've put up. What a polite neighbor you are!

Part Five: After the sale

Congratulations! You did it! Pat yourself on the back, have a tasty beverage of your choice, get some sleep.

Now you just have a little bit of aftermath to contend with. Visually assess what remains from the sale. Depending on how much is left and what your goals are, you can use one or more of the techniques below to clear everything out:

- Pick out items or groups of items to sell online, at a local live auction, to a dealer, or at a consignment store (see "Selling things everywhere except an estate sale" on page 10).

- Bring in people you know to take things for free. There are a lot of people in situations where free household goods (for their own use, to sell, or to send to family) are a huge boon. People new to the area just getting settled, friends with close church/synagogue/mosque communities which do charity work, and college students are prime contenders.

- Donate items to a charity. You may know a local/independent organization that can use your stuff, or try one of the big players that will (usually) pick up your donation:
  - » Goodwill (Goodwill.org)
  - » Salvation Army (SalvationArmyUSA.org)[9]
  - » AMVETS (Amvets.org)
  - » Habitat for Humanity (Habitat.org)
  - » The Arc (feelgreatdonate.org)

- At some point in the process, you may want to trash everything that's left. Google what's available in your local area. You should be able to find places where you can rent a dumpster or dumpster bag (that will later be picked up) or places that come and do a cleanout (for a larger fee).

- If you're feeling more ambitious and or have the time, you can try creating an ad on craigslist (or your local equivalent) offering to give everything that's left to someone willing to

---

9 This organization has a troubling history of anti-LGBT policies which, as of this writing, it claims to have reformed (see bit.ly/sa-out). Please do your due diligence when working with any non-profit.

come and take it all. If you have enough decent stuff left, you may even try charging for your "take it all" estate sale remnants.

That's just about it. You can move on to whatever you need to do to wrap up, be it cleaning (or hiring cleaners), putting the property on the market, arranging for the property to be torn down, moving out, dealing with estate legalities or whatever else.

Conclusion

You can do it! (Or, you can choose not to, and hire someone to do it for you.) But I do hope that all the preceding info will ease your way, whatever you choose. Good luck with your sale!

Afterword: Lockdown Variations

I like to think that this book will be read and used in a world where we can go into buildings and mingle with other humans safely — but 2020 has shown that this is not always the case. In the wake of lockdowns and other safety measures necessitated by COVID-19, traditional estate sale and auction companies have rushed to put together viable online solutions for selling the contents of estates. There are also other online services which have been around for some time but have suddenly become more attractive options as good old in-person estate sales have become less practical.

If you need to sell the contents of an estate and the conditions are such that you can't hold a traditional in-person sale, there are some safer options. Please assess the current conditions carefully before deciding on which methods are the most prudent.

Estatesales.net

You can advertise your sale on the same way described in the *Making your estatesales.net ad* section in Part Three, but instead of having an open house, take appointments via phone, text, or email. Only allow a one party or pod of people into the sale at a time.

Estatesales.net has also started offering options to list your items for sale directly on their website. This, of course, means taking pictures clear enough that someone can make a buying decision from internet viewing alone. That may not be as high bar as you think though — check out the other pictures already up there. They're not intimidatingly professional. You should be fine with a cell phone camera and some of the photo tips described in the *Taking Photos* section of Part Three. If you choose to sell your items online on estatesales.net, you can specify "local pickup only" and/or offer shipping. Most people seem to choose to do only the former.

If you do offer pickup, set up separate times with buyers and make sure to put the appropriate safety protocols in place.

Auctions

You may choose to turn over some or all of the estate contents to an auctioneer who will sell everything online (or in-person, or both).

The best approach to finding an auction/auctioneer is through word-of-mouth, as reputation counts for a lot in this business. If you don't happen to know anyone who knows anyone, however, you can look for auctioneers in your area on auctionzip.com and then do whatever due diligence you can by asking around and checking out Yelp, the Better Business Bureau or any other resources germane to your area.

During the pandemic, auctions have been increasingly held online, even by auction houses which used to operate solely in-person. There are several methodologies for online auctions of this sort, and several popular online places where they take place. If you poke around these sites, you can get a feel for them:

- auctionzip.com
- liveauctioneers.com
- proxibid.com
- hibid.com
- invaluable.com

Some online auctions take place live, with a streamed video feed of the auctioneer augmented with software which shows the bids real time. Some omit the auctioneer and the software runs the whole shebang automatically. Others are asynchronous and allow users to bid up to a certain date and time when each item ends (somewhat like eBay). There are also hybrid models that involve bidding in-person and online. What's best for your stuff and situation will depend more on finding a good auctioneer who knows what they're doing than the format — though they may recommend one method over another depending on what you've got.

EBTH (everything but the house)

This site (ebth.com) offers both full service and more DIY options for holding an online auction. Since they specialize in estate liquidations, their packages will be more of tailored solution with significantly more guidance. There will be fees that you wouldn't have with a completely DIY sale, but this could still be a good option for times when a DIY in-person sale isn't possible.

For all of these solutions involving outside help, there will be fees associated with the auction house's cut of the proceeds and possibly some expenses and/or logistics involved with getting items to them or photographed. These are solutions for the COVID era, when time is of the essence — not necessarily the most lucrative or DIY options.

As DIY as possible

You may wish take a hybrid approach, only sending select items to an auction-house-run auction and doing the rest yourself. Or, if you have the time, space, and ambition, selling everything yourself online.

Of course, you can sell almost anything on eBay, but you may wish to look at what you have to sell vis-a-vis the strengths and weaknesses of various online selling platforms. Each will have different methodologies for listing, following through on transactions, fees (or not), shipping (or not), etc. Some I recommend checking out:

- **eBay** (ebay.com)
- **Mercari** for household goods, clothes, collectibles, etc (mercari.com)
- **TheRealReal** for high-end fashion (therealreal.com)
- **Swap.com** for clothes and some accessories, especially in bulk — this is consignment, not an auction (swap.com)
- **Thredup** for clothes and some accessories — again, consignment not an auction (thredup.com)
- **Facebook Marketplace** for pretty much anything, especially for large items and/or local sales (facebook.com)
- **Facebook Groups** for pretty much anything — look for a "buy and sell" group in the niche you're selling in (facebook.com)
- **Craigslist** or **Kajiji** for pretty much anything, usually local (craigslist.com and kajiji.ca)

Good luck with your sale, and stay safe!

Please visit **EstatesaleDIY.com** for bonus material & resources.

www.ingramcontent.com/pod-product-compliance
Lightning Source LLC
Chambersburg PA
CBHW071608200326
41519CB00021BB/6927